D1458050

PLAY ON WORDS

RANDOM
HOUSE NEW YORK

For Stopher,
For Jamie,
For Phil and
For Mike,

For Libby,
For Mary,
For Patty,
For Jane,

For George and
For Walter,
For Whatzis name?

For Donna,
For Annie,
For Karen, too.

For Catherine,
For Nancy,
For Karen, again.

For Jean Ives, Giovanni,
For M. C. Domandi,

For Lizzy,
For Jeannie,
For Mary Lou,

For Josie,
For Carol, for Clinto,
For

____

Sign your name here

Copyright © 1972 by Alice and Martin Provensen

All rights reserved under International and Pan-American Copyright Conventions. Published in the United States by Random House, Inc., New York, and simultaneously in Canada by Random House of Canada Limited, Toronto.

Library of Congress Cataloging in Publication Data

Provensen, Alice.
Play on words.

SUMMARY: Brief text and illustrations introduce a variety of games with sounds and meanings of words.
1. Word games—Juvenile literature. [1. Word games. 2. Picture books] I. Provensen, Martin, joint author. II. Title.
GV1507.W8P7 793.7'3 [E] 72-1585
ISBN 0-394-82124-6
ISBN 0-394-92124-0 (lib. ed.)

Manufactured in the United States of America

FOREWORD

TO PLAY is to have fun.

TO PLAY is to join in a game, to make a joke, to amuse oneself.

There is a lot to be said for play.

WORDS are what we say.

WORDS are what we read.

There is a lot to be said FOR WORDS.

A word has a sound,

a meaning, a size, a shape.

TO PLAY ON WORDS is to have fun with words.

TO PLAY ON WORDS is to play tricks with words, to hide words in words, to play jokes with the sound and the meaning and the size and the shape of a word, to use the same word in two senses.

Watch out for words!

SOME WORDS make sense.

SOME WORDS make no cents.

This foreword has three more (not four) words:

LETTUCE GO FORWARD.

Easy Words

Z-Z-Z-Z-Z
R-R-R-R

M-M-M
R-R-R-R
S-S-S-S
S-S-S-S

Ho-Ho Homonyms

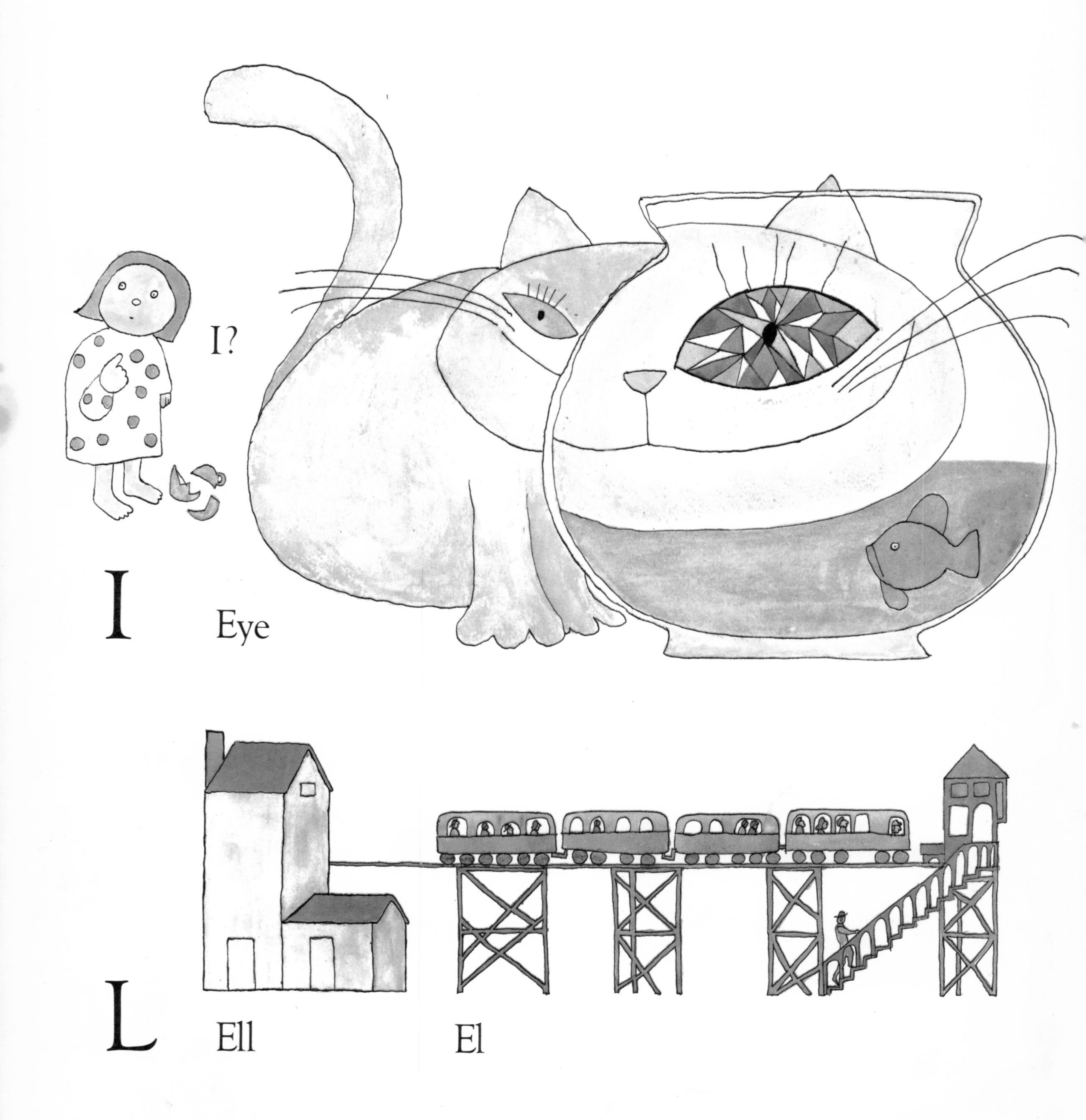

B
Bee
BB
C
See
Sea
Seesaw
U
You
Ewe
Yew
Yoo-hoo!
T
Tea
Tee
Tee-hee

O, O, oh-oh!

Bow Bow Bobo

Dough Doe Dodo

Tow Toe Toto

Sew
So-So
So
and
So!
No
Know
No, No!
Row,
Roe,
Row your boat
What Ho?
Land Hoe
Ho, Ho, Ho!

EXercises

X means kisses

X means incorrect

X means multiply

X marks the spot

means stop, look and listen

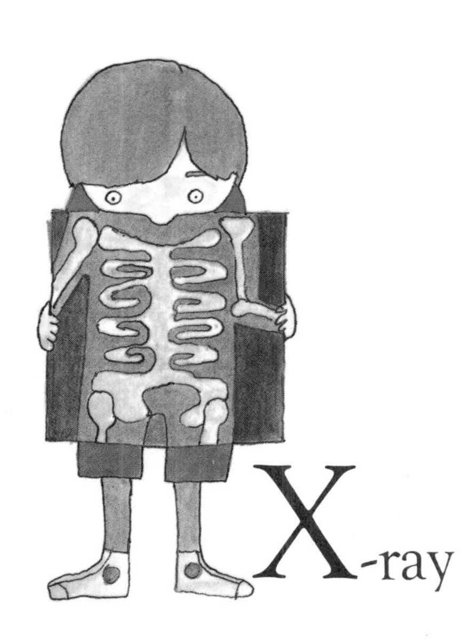

X-ray

X means 10

How many are X little Indians?

X is a choice

X is the winner

X means crossed out

X means sign on the dotted line

Noisy Words

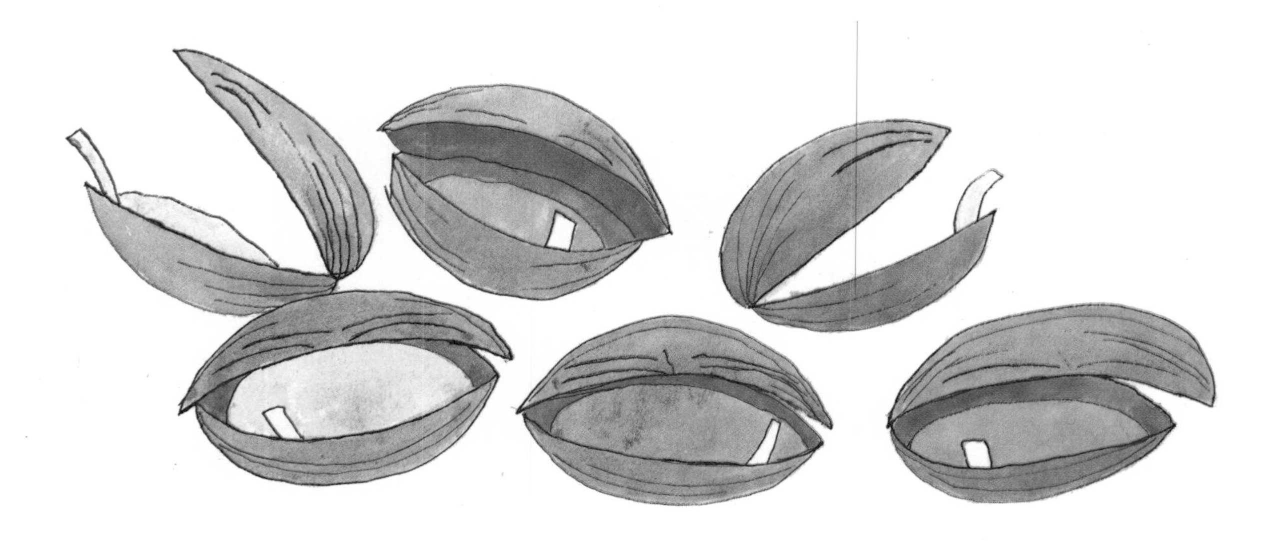

A Clamoring

A Yammering

A Terrible Din

Watch Words

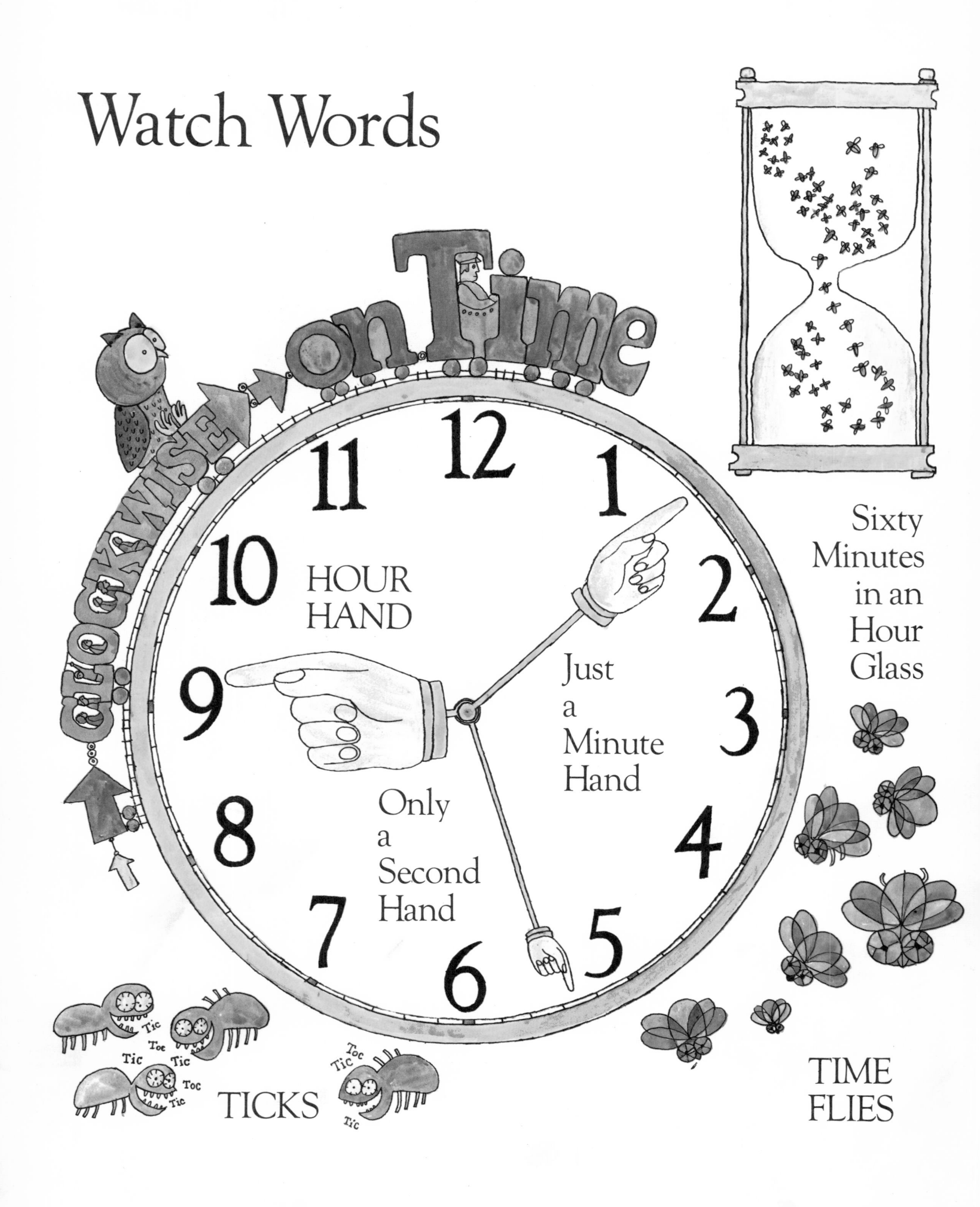

CLOCKWISE
on Time
12
1
2
3
4
5
6
7
8
9
10
11
HOUR HAND
Just a Minute Hand
Only a Second Hand
Sixty Minutes in an Hour Glass
Tic
Toc
Tic
Tic
Toc
Tic
Tic
Toc
Tic
TICKS
TIME FLIES

Watch Out For Words

WORDS in a Word

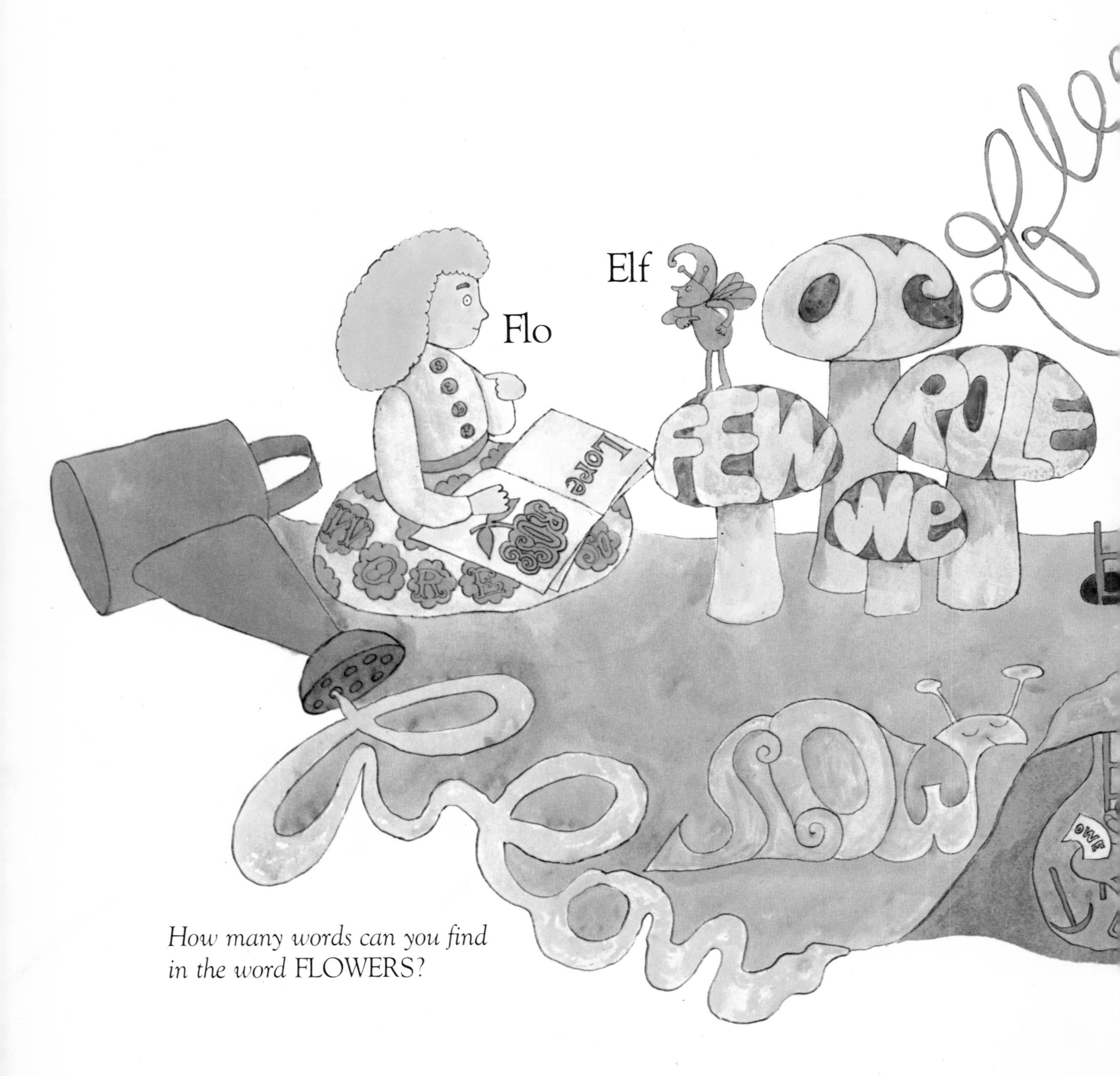

How many words can you find in the word FLOWERS?

OWERS
Owe
sew
sore
woe
worse
ROW
SOW
low
lower

4 words more

FOUR sheets in the wind

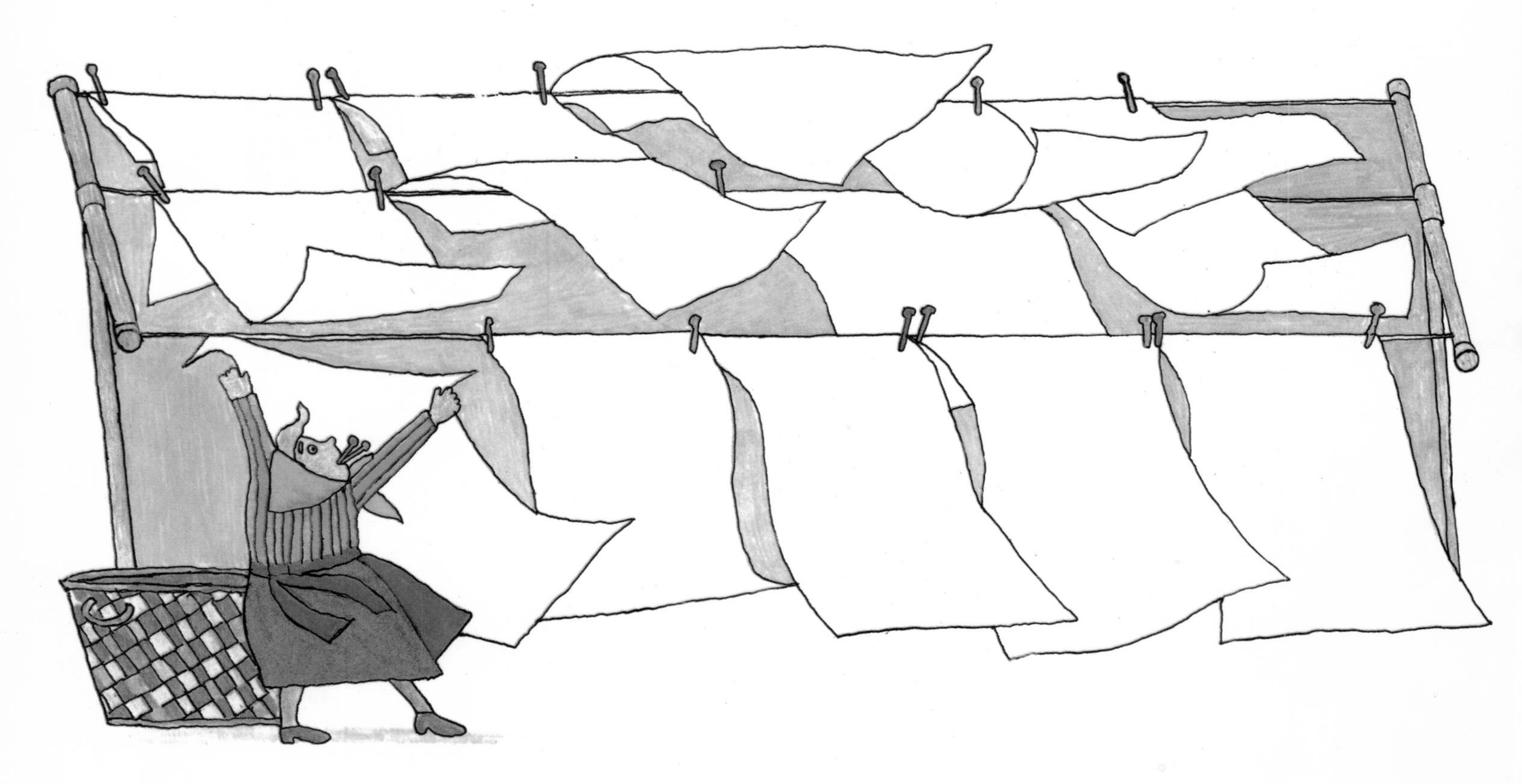

FOURTEEN sheets in the wind

The Glorious FOURTH

FORTY thieves

Words in Time

Words in Space

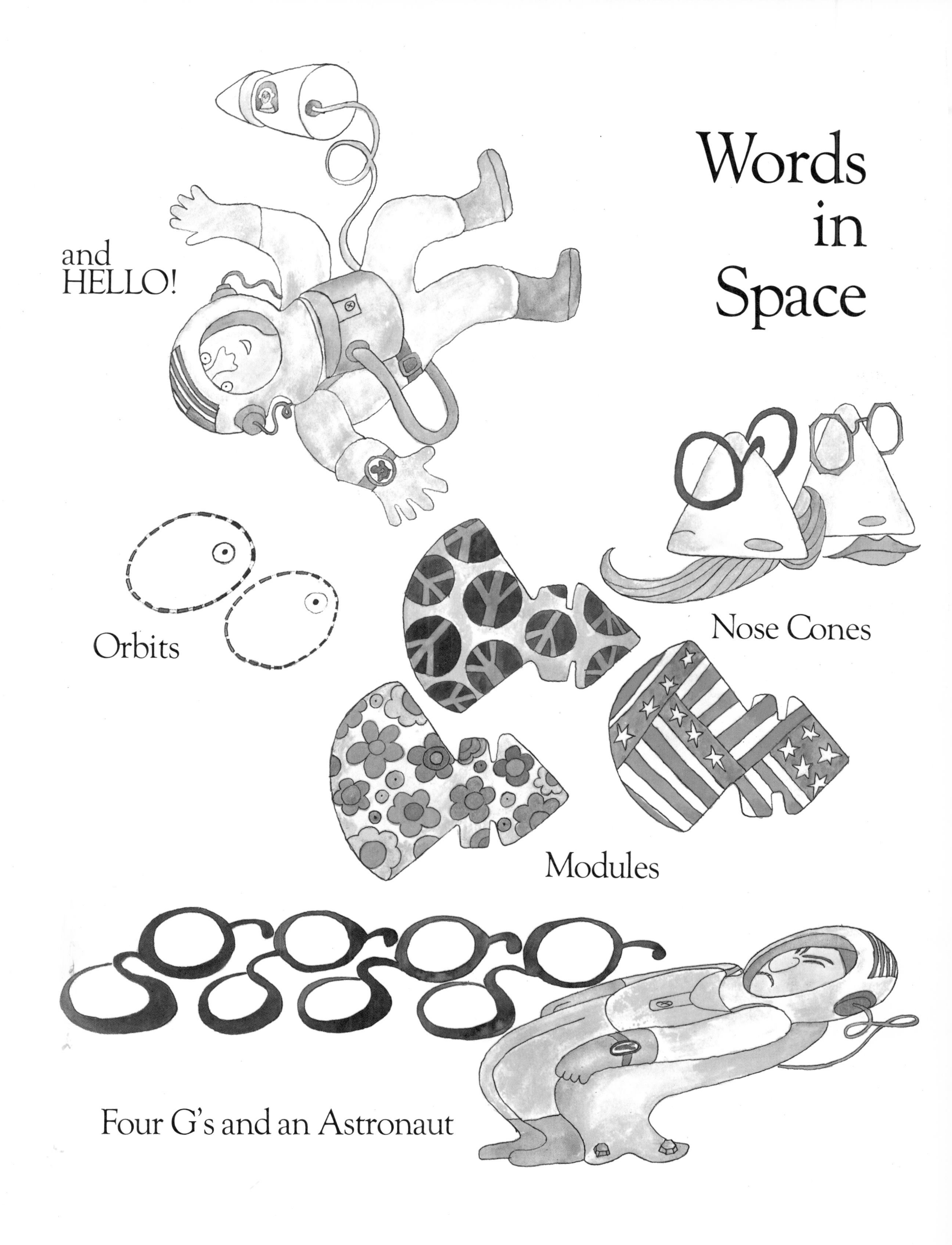

WORDS and
Words all over the place

TISEMENT
STOP
GO
NO EXIT
ONE WAY
DEAD END
car
bus
Motorcycle
car
car
automobile

Say yes

Say yes, please

Say no

Say no, thank you

Y, oh why so noisy, O

YO HO
YO HO
YO HO
YOICKS
Yuk
Yirr

Yawn
Yaulp
Yawp
Yaff
Yaff
Yip
Yelp
Yelp
Yawl
Yaul
Yaup
Yikes

Famous Last Words

He who laughs last
laughs last.

YAK
YAK

YUK
YUK

Heard words Unheard-of words
Absurd words
Down words Up words
Upside-down words Front and
Back words
Before and **Afterword.**

Did you find ALL of these words in the flowers?

Flo, elf, or, few, role, we, lore, rose, wore, SO,
ore, self, flow, slow, owe, ow, low, lower, SEW,
worse, row, owl, fowl, slew, sore, woe, SOW.

Did you find these words ALL over the place?

advertisement, sign, movie, hotel, market, in, CAR,
fire, smoke, soot, smog, exit, choo-choo, CAR,
stop, dead, end, cycle, van, bus, way, CAR,
R.R.X. motor, go, no, one, AUTOMOBILE.

Did you hear that terrible din?

Boom, blast, swoosh, Ah-ooo-gah, RRR-ZZZ-RR,
Clank, blah-blah, whirr, zoing, zoing, zoing, crump,
Honk, honk, rattle, rattle, crash, BEEP, BEEP.